Gourd Art Basics

The Complete Guide to
Cleaning, Preparation, & Repair

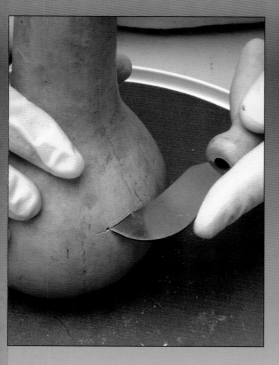

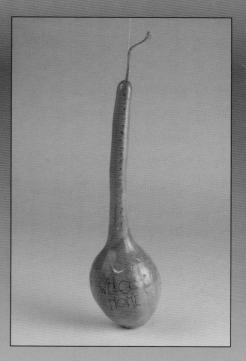

C. Angela Mohr

Schiffer Publishing Ltd

4880 Lower Valley Road   Atglen, Pennsylvania 19310

Dedication

This book is dedicated to my brother, Rick Mohr, tool and technique innovator. When stuck for a tool or an easier way to accomplish the task at hand, I would just call Rick and by golly he comes up with an idea. It takes a creative spirit to pull bits of unrelated information together and come up with an entirely new and useful solution. Rick tells me there is always an easier way of doing something, and I believe him.

COVER PICTURE CAPTION:
Shown is a finished bowl that was made from a gourd that had a crack extending from its rim and was repaired.

Other Schiffer Books by C. Angela Mohr:
Making Gourd Ornaments, 978-0-7643-2716-2, $12.95

Other Schiffer Books on Related Subjects
Decorating Gourds: Carving, Burning, Painting and More, 0-7643-1312-6, $14.95

Copyright © 2008 by C. Angela Mohr
Library of Congress Control Number: 2007937646

Designed by Mark David Bowyer
Type set in Garamond Ultra Condensed/ Humanist521 BT

ISBN: 978-0-7643-2829-9
Printed in China

Schiffer Books are available at special discounts for bulk purchases for sales promotions or premiums. Special editions, including personalized covers, corporate imprints, and excerpts can be created in large quantities for special needs. For more information contact the publisher:

Published by Schiffer Publishing Ltd.
4880 Lower Valley Road
Atglen, PA 19310
Phone: (610) 593-1777; Fax: (610) 593-2002
E-mail: Info@schifferbooks.com

For the largest selection of fine reference books on this and related subjects,
please visit our website at: **www.schifferbooks.com**
We are always looking for people to write books on new and related subjects.
If you have an idea for a book, please contact us at:
proposals@schifferbooks.com

This book may be purchased from the publisher.
Include $5.00 for shipping.
Please try your bookstore first.
You may write for a free catalog.

In Europe, Schiffer books are distributed by
Bushwood Books
6 Marksbury Ave.
Kew Gardens
Surrey TW9 4JF England
Phone: 44 (0) 20 8392 8585; Fax: 44 (0) 20 8392 9876
E-mail: info@bushwoodbooks.co.uk
Website: www.bushwoodbooks.co.uk

What's Inside

Introduction

So, you've got your hands on a gourd…Now what? Here is a guide to basics you can learn and build upon for years of "gourding" pleasure! Learn how to recognize dehydrated gourds, how to clean them up, open them, gut them, and prepare them for all the art and craft projects you can imagine. Learn how to repair unfortunate accidents.

Using readily available tools and supplies already in your home or garage, gourd fun can begin right now! Today! Later on, try some of the power tool tricks for really big fun.

This book goes beyond many how-to methods for gourd enthusiasts by providing detailed step-by-step information for accomplishing preparation tasks with different strategies: basic handwork to more elaborate power tool methods. A solid and thorough foundation for future ideas and projects!

Part One:

Getting the Gourds

How wonderful that you have the gourd fever! Now, to get your hands on some gourds and learn basic techniques for preparing them for art and craft projects. First, understand there are several terms bandied about for useable art/craft gourds: dehydrated gourds, dried-out gourds, 'cured' gourds. All these terms mean the same thing—the moisture content of the gourd (the bulk of its weight) is gone and the basic structure of the gourd wall is all that is left, along with some seeds and internal connective tissue called pith.

If you grow gourds, you know they prosper on a vine all summer, looking green and feeling heavy. In the fall when the vine dies and the gourd is harvested, dehydrating begins and continues through the next couple seasons. At some point, you will begin to second-guess the viability of those gourds because of their molded, grungy appearance. Some will look pretty nasty! The moisture inside the gourd evaporates through the skin and stem and in the process mold will grow on the exterior surface. However, if by the following spring or summer, the gourds have held their shape, are light for their size, and rattle with seeds, they should be ready to clean up for a brighter future. At that point they will be hard and brown or tan colored under all the grunge and mold.

There are many ways to prepare a gourd for a project and frankly, every gourd enthusiast will perfect his or her own strategies...some elaborate and some primitive, depending on such factors as purpose, available tools, and even how many gourds needing to be prepared at once. I approach a bunch of gourds commando-style—getting the job done with whatever is available. I use what I have had in the garage for ages and encourage you to do the same. There is plenty of time to investigate all the great gadgets on the market later. For now, get a handle on the basics, then set up procedures based on what you have around your house and what handy tools you can purchase in your area.

Noticing the Details

When first looking through the gourd pile, take a moment to examine the grunge (meaning dirt, dead skin, bug carcasses, etc.) and mold on the gourds. We will work with a couple gourd molds you may come in contact with because I believe a working knowledge of molds not only makes the cleaning efficient, but it is also the beginning of good gourd inspection and wise gourd purchases (if you choose to buy from others at local farmer markets or gardening swaps). Some molds are just easier to clean than others and why invite more work if there is an easier path, right? We will be working with two basic exterior situations: 1) a sooty, grainy mold that cleans relatively easily; and 2) a waxy, skin-mold that is not actually wax or mold at all. Rather, it's the result of gourd skin that underwent some kind of mutation during the dehydration process and formed a watertight seal encasing the gourd.

Various molds

When I first began producing gourd art, I decided I would rather grow and clean my own gourds for the thrill of saying my finished piece was touched by my hands only. Years later, a little of that thrill is gone in lieu of spending my time doing the art, but I still wash plenty of gourds each season and there is still a delight in seeing a yucky gourd come to life as the filth is scrubbed and rinsed away. There's nothing like it! Do I still choose to clean and use a gourd with a waxy, skin-mold? Yes, if it is my last gourd or if it is the right shape or size…otherwise, I avoid them if I can. However, knowledge is power, so you too will learn how to clean this kind of surface crud.

After you have chosen the gourd you want to work with based on your design idea, critically assess it for holes, crack lines, or warty spots. These imperfections indicate weakened or thin gourd walls and can be areas of concern if you have a particular design in mind. They will certainly indicate extra repair work if you do decide to use the gourd for a project. (See Repairing the Accidents.)

Shown are the two molds we will be working with in the book.

The wall's thickness will sometimes determine a design's potential and what kind of tools will be needed to complete the project. A thick wall will need power tools, whereas a thinner wall might only require a handsaw or carpet knife. Knock on a gourd with your knuckle. Does it sound substantial? Gently press the wall with your thumbs to see if it has any give to it at all. As a learning opportunity, compare a flawed gourd with a sound one: find a cracked gourd in the pile and tap it; then tap a solid one for com-

parison. Over time you will be able to discern differences easily.

Overall, preparing a gourd for craft or art projects involves cleaning the exterior (including the stem), opening it, and finishing the interior depending on what the final product is supposed to be. For example, opening a gourd for a birdhouse, which does not need a complete clear out, is different than preparing a gourd interior for a jar. It may be the same type of gourd, but the approach is different based on intent.

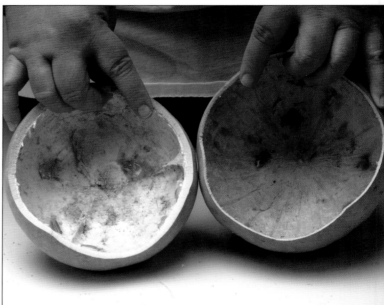

Wall thicknesses

Equipping for the Job

A comment or two about tools and equipment: As I stated earlier, I heartily encourage the use of tools and supplies already in your home. Yes, there are many wonderful tools in the world and you will eventually invest in a vast array of gadgets, but see what can be done with what you have on hand first. Once you have a feel for the job, look around for neat tools and gadgets. In this book, I show a couple ways to do the same skill…from the basic, on-the-cheap tools I used at first to get the job done, to the more elaborate discoveries I made later on. You will certainly come up with ideas on your own.

Two items I highly encourage are latex gloves and respiration masks. Gourds are round and will slip under your hands. Latex gloves will help you maintain a good grip on the gourd as you work. As for respiration masks: gourd dust is toxic for its mold spores and for its fine texture. Once inhaled, it can wreak havoc with sinuses, bronchial tubes, and lungs. Do yourself a favor and get a $30 two-canister respirator from your local hardware or paint store and if at all possible, work outside in a breeze. I wear a two-canister respirator, safety glasses over my eyeglasses, and sometimes a netted gnat hat over everything. A hospital mask is probably fine if gutting or sanding only one gourd. However, one mask will never be enough to hold back the dust once you have the gourd fever and are working on several gourds at once. So, for your safety, forewarned is forearmed!

As you can tell, some of the tools below are duplicates, but it is good to see the possibilities. Before investing in anything, look around your home and see what is available. My spinning lazy susan came from a kitchen cabinet after I emptied the contents into a box. The box is easier to slide in and out of the cabinet when I use the herbs and spices, and I can spin a gourd easier when I'm cutting it open. Be creative. Be a gourder!

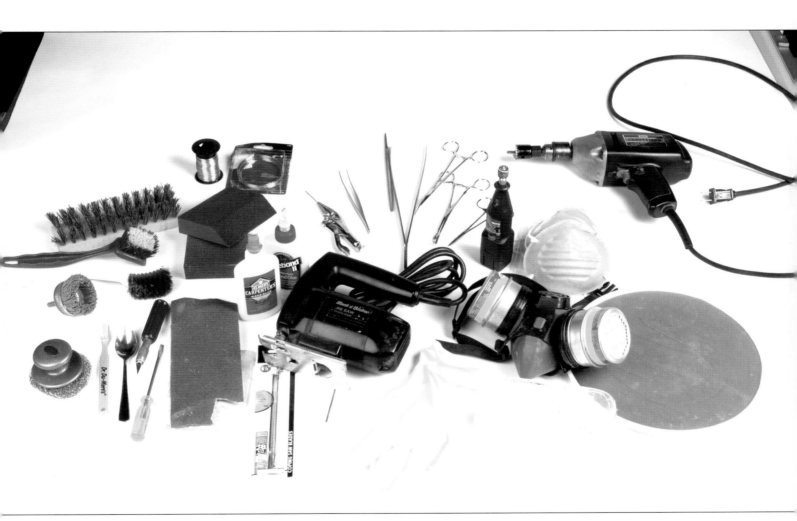

The tools in the foreground are my mainstays when preparing gourds: a metal pot scrubbie, a toothbrush, a grapefruit spoon, Xacto knife, a flathead screwdriver, Sandblaster sandpaper – non-clogging and, since it is brightly colored, can be located on the workbench easily, wood glue, a jigsaw with coping saw blades, latex gloves, a two-canister respirator, safety goggles, and a lazy susan with a rubber lining. Everything else in the background is a variation of these things, plus some power equipment we will review later.

Part Two:

Cleaning the Outside

Sooty, Grainy Mold

For exterior cleaning of sooty, grainy molds, you will need access to water and a scrubbing device such as the kind used for cleaning pots, a sanding sponge, or a stiff brush. Wear latex gloves to save your hands from constant water exposure and the scraping effects of your scrubbing tool. Some folks also use 1:10 bleach to water solution. I have not found that to be worth the time or smell, but please explore that option if you have trouble with mold spores. I work outside generally, so spores are not a concern.

Although we are cleaning one gourd at a time here, when cleaning many, many gourds in one session, nothing surpasses the summer/backyard treatment of filling a black plastic trash bag with gourds, hosing them thoroughly, tying the bag shut, and leaving it in the sun to steam. Turn the bag several times, and by golly, when those gourds come out, their grunge and mold have been softened and wash away quickly!

Let's start!

Begin by choosing a gourd that appears to be dirty all over with black, sooty mold.

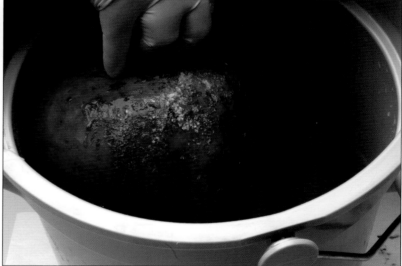

Rinse it with hot water to help the mold, skin flakes, and dirt loosen their grip. Room temperature water works fine, but the heat in hot water just speeds things up a bit.

Once the gourd has been wet for a while, scrub the exterior surface and dip the gourd in water; this will allow a fine trickle of water to run over the gourd and rinse off the loosened crud.

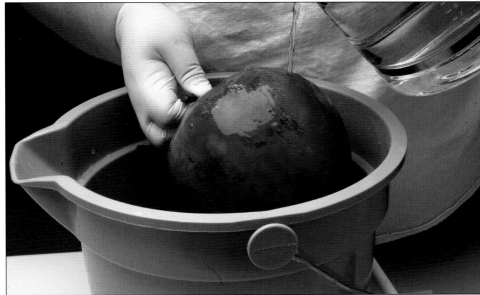

Rinsing away the crud will expose the missed areas because the water will catch onto pieces of debris and make ripples.

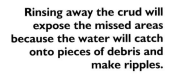

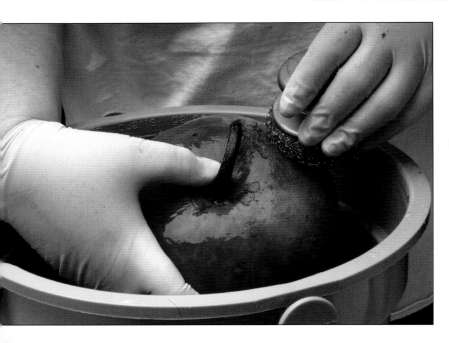

Continue scrubbing the missed areas.

Rinse again, looking for missed bits of crud. The goal will be a smooth sheet of water running over a cleaned gourd surface without ripples.

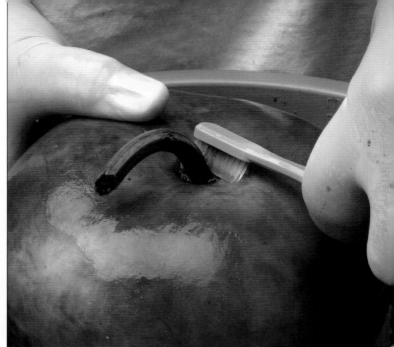

Clean the crevice where the stem attaches to the gourd. In this tight area, a toothbrush is handy.

A clean stem is the telltale sign of a thorough job. Rub the scrubbie over the length of the stem with one hand while supporting the opposite side of the stem with the other hand.

The mottled coloration on the gourd wall is normal and is produced by the molds that grow on the gourd surface as it was dehydrating. The marks cannot be bleached away since they are part of the wall. They can be covered by paint, but interesting mottling can be a highly prized part of a gourd project.

Waxy, Skin-like Mold

Waxy, skin-like mold results in a challenging surface crud that, depending on your purposes, may not be worth the time to clean because the surface seems to be encased in a waterproofed seal. Do not back down! This is actually gourd skin that underwent some kind of mutation during dehydration and stuck to the gourd's exterior. It needs to be cleaned off because it will not accept art techniques easily and will eventually flake in places, ruining whatever you decide to do with the gourd. Running water and scrubbies are still needed, but add a dull table or paring knife to your bag of tricks and don't bother with a sanding sponge (it will only glide over the waxy surface without getting the bite it needs to dig into the crud).

Let's go!

Using a table or paring knife, scrape multiple lines through the waxy stuff to produce a lot of entry places for the water.

Start by pouring **HOT** water over the gourd. In this instance, hot water will be your friend because the heat will soften the skin enough for an initial scraping.

Pour more **HOT** water over the gourd.

After another 15 minutes or so, try your metal pot scrubbie and see what you can get off.

Keep rinsing…

…and keep scrubbing.

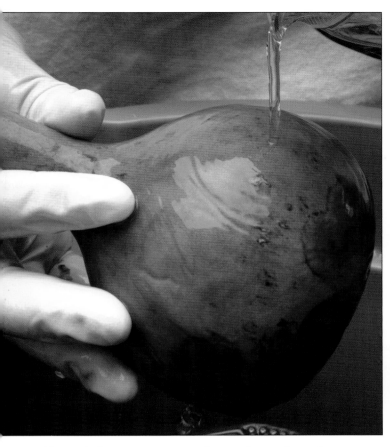

When rinsing, pay close attention to places where the water catches and ripples instead of running smoothly. This kind of mold is pale and not easily seen.

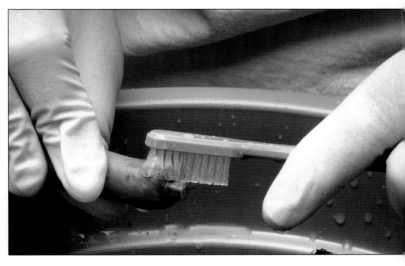

Cleaning the stem end is easier! Just follow the procedure we used before of supporting the back of the stem with one hand as you run the scrubbie lengthwise along the stem. Unfortunately, this stem broke—but the nub still needs to be cleaned.

Continue until the water runs smoothly over the gourd surface. Usually, three hot water soaks coupled with a metal scrubbie and elbow grease will clear the waxy skin-like mold away.

Everything is clean and ready to go!

Part Three:

Opening the Gourds

After the cleaned gourds have dried, it's time to open them up! The tools used will depend on the thickness of the gourd wall. Thick walls need power tools because the denseness resembles a soft wood, whereas a thin wall does not have as much material to cut through so a handsaw or knife will work. Since I know where my gourds come from and what they were like in the past, I generally have a good idea of what I've got my hands on. You will learn the subtleties of your stash as time goes on as well. Start minimally, then build to bigger, more powerful tools as needed.

Hand Tools

Thin-walled gourds will give way with gentle thumb pressure against the outside—there will be a little give. They open easily with hand tools such as a carpet knife or handsaw. I have a homemade saw my brother made by snapping a coping saw blade in half with wire cutting pliers and securing a piece of it into the jaws of a locking wrench. The handle is sturdy, the blade is fine toothed, and I saved money by not buying another tool.

Let's cut!

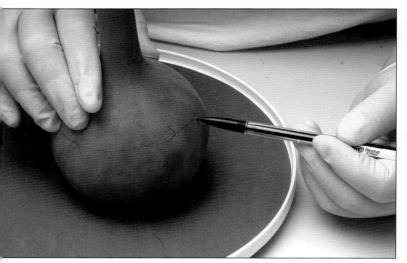

Mark a pencil line around the gourd as a cutting guideline by rotating the gourd as you hold a pencil against the surface.

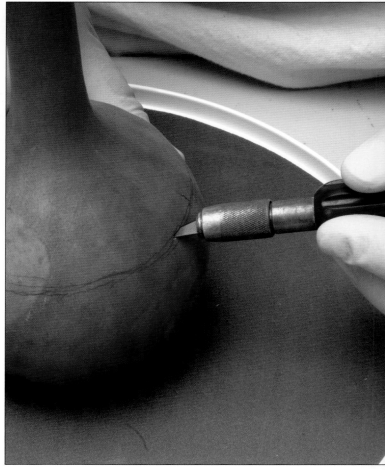

Make a small opening place in the gourd with an Xacto knife. You may be able to use the Xacto to cut the gourd open, but at least get the opening.

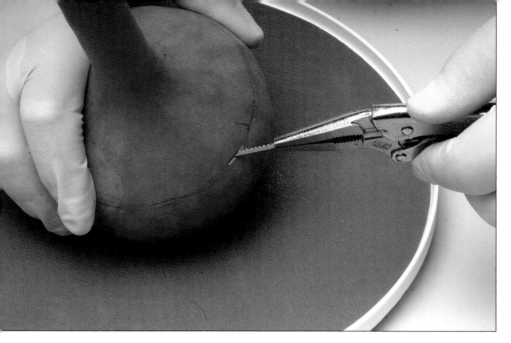

Insert your cutting blade into the opening. I am using my homemade saw.

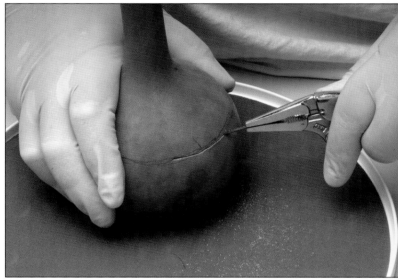

Using a sawing motion, move around the circumference until the original line is met.

Take the top off.

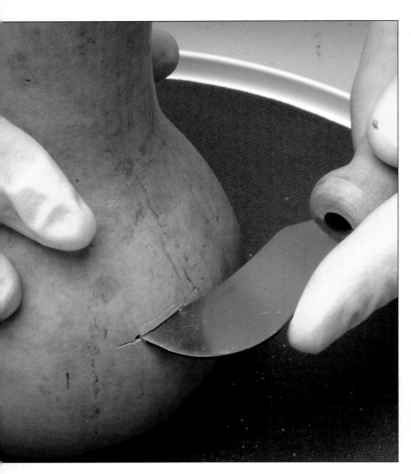

Jigsaw

Mostly, I use an inexpensive jigsaw I got as an engagement gift from my husband twenty-five years ago. (Don't laugh, I also got a ring and a formal set of gold flat ware for twelve—he says he wanted to hit all the bases!) I try to use the finest woodworking blade I can find at my local Ace Hardware or Wal-Mart, which is a coping saw blade I snap in half (thereby getting two blades!). The blade probably makes little difference if all I'm doing is getting the top off the gourd, but if I am opening a gourd for a lidded jar, I do not want much of the gourd wall to disappear in the cutting line. A large blade can eat up as much as 1/8" of wall, making the lid sit askew from the bottom. The smaller and finer the blade, the less amount of gourd material that will disappear when the blade moves through the gourd wall. Coping saw blades are cheap, cut a nice line, and do not eat up much gourd wall in the process.

Let's get "gourding"!

If you use a knife instead of a saw, score the cutting line by going over and over it several times. Be patient and the knife will cut all the way through the wall.

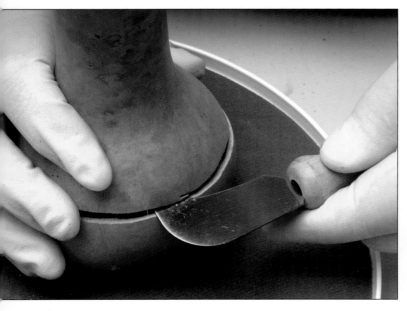

Continue cutting in slow, sawing movements around the gourd until you meet the starting point.

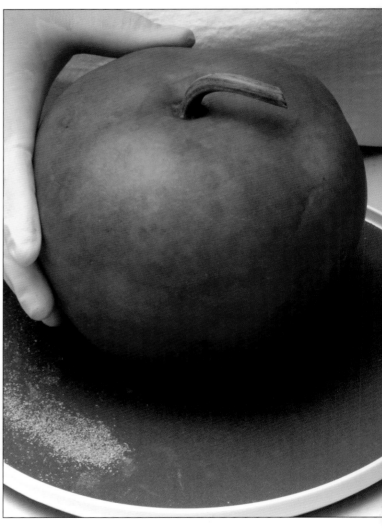

Start the process by wearing latex gloves for a good grip and sitting the gourd on a nonslip surface such as this lazy susan with the rubber lining. Gourds are round, and no matter how firmly you think you are holding a gourd, it will slip.

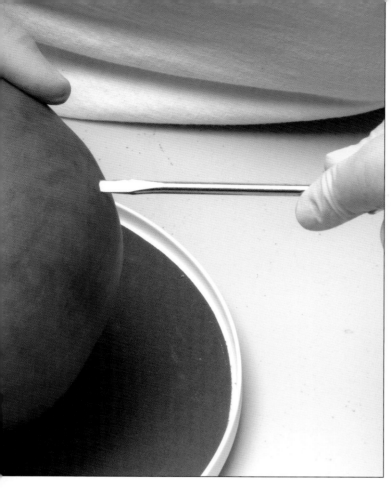

Push a knife or flathead screwdriver into the wall where the cutting line will be.

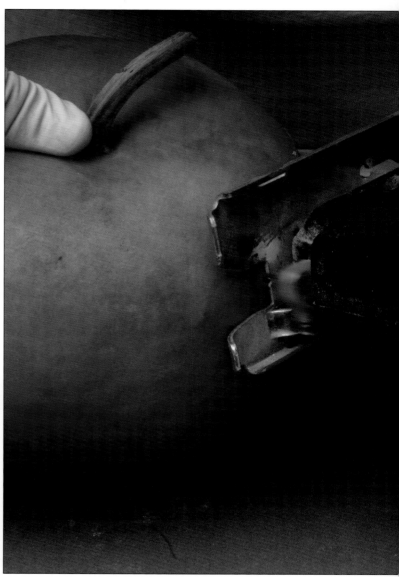

Start the jigsaw and turn the gourd with one hand while cutting with the other. If you are opening this gourd for a lidded jar, cut a wavy line, beveling the jigsaw blade up and then down once as you go so the lid will nestle onto the curves instead of slipping off a flat rim.

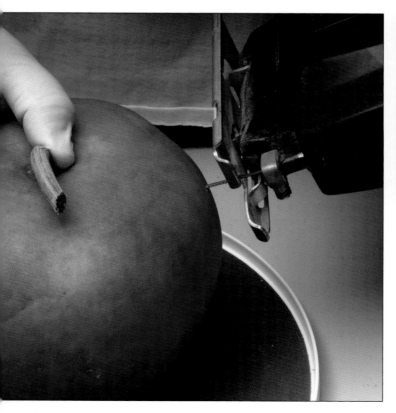

Standing over the gourd, wedge the jigsaw blade into it.

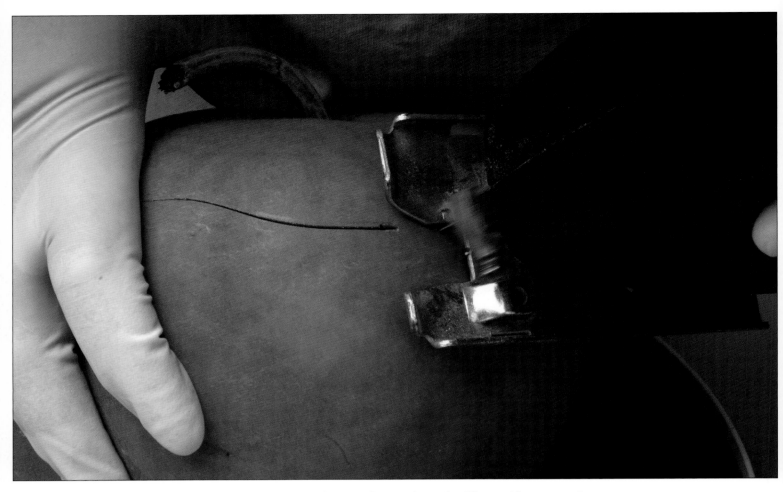

If you have a variable speed jigsaw, slow it down as it nears the starting point. The goal is to meet the starting point in a smooth line.

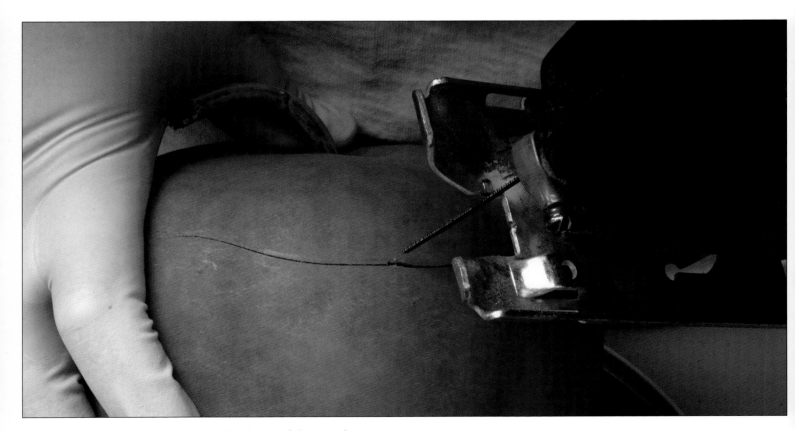

Turn off the jigsaw and pull the blade out of the gourd.

Remove the top.

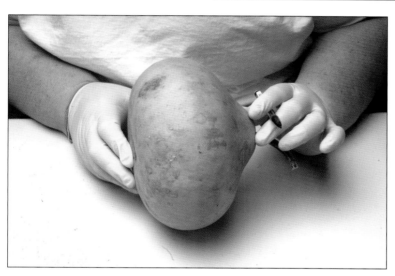

To cut a gourd open for a bowl – where a leveled rim is desired – grab a pencil and a gourd with a flat bottom.

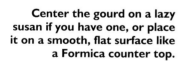

Center the gourd on a lazy susan if you have one, or place it on a smooth, flat surface like a Formica counter top.

Hold the pencil tightly with your elbow pinned against your body so the pencil stays stationary. Turn the gourd, holding the pencil in the same position against the exterior wall so it makes a level line on the gourd surface.

Insert a knife on the line to make an opening.

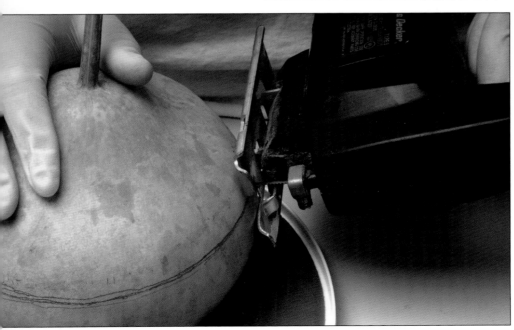

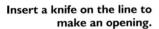

Insert the jigsaw blade into the opening.

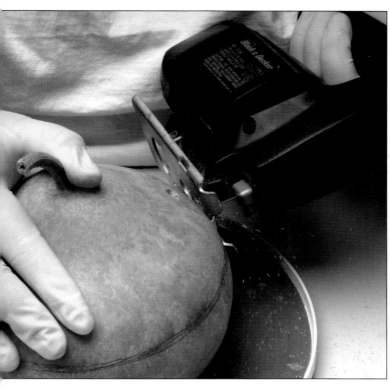

Turn off the jigsaw and take the blade out of the gourd.

Holding the jigsaw arm still, with the elbow pinned against your body, turn it on and rotate the gourd into the jigsaw blade. The goal here is to make the cutting line as level as possible so holding the jigsaw stationary will help.

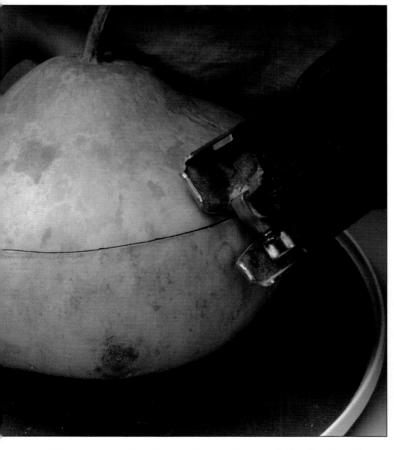

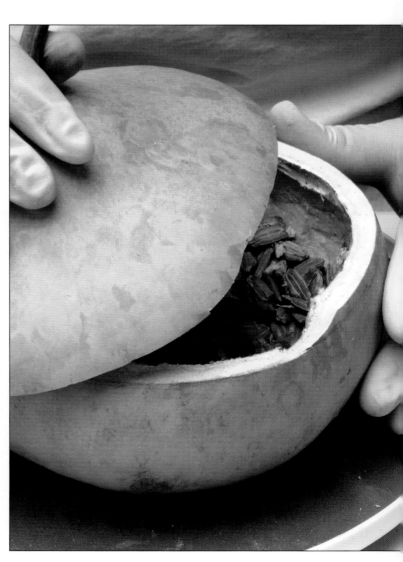

When approaching the starting point, carefully align the blade with the beginning so you can meet it with a smooth line.

Take the top off the gourd.

Bandsaw

A bandsaw is a great way to get a leveled, flat rim for a bowl because the blade cuts straight across the gourd from one side to the other. Although a bandsaw is not a finishing tool, it is handy if you have many gourds to open fast—one swipe and it's a done deal. The rim on a gourd opened with a bandsaw will not be completely level every time, but once cut it is cut. It's a fast tool perfect for making bowls because of its ability to cut a flat, straight line but it is also the most dangerous tool you can use because of its power and, therefore, its inability to discriminate between a gourd and a finger. If you have any doubts at all, ask a local carpenter or handyman to open a bunch of gourds for you. The finishing can be done at home. Otherwise, use the jigsaw or a knife to get the most level cut you can muster.

Let's be careful!

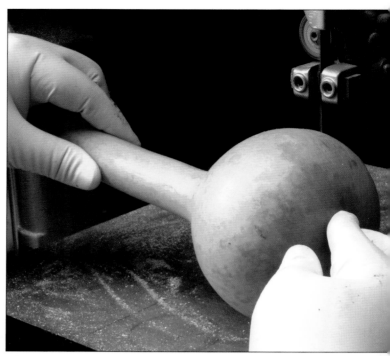

Hold opposite sides of the gourd, keeping your fingers away from the blade. A bandsaw is not a precision tool; you will not be working close to the blade.

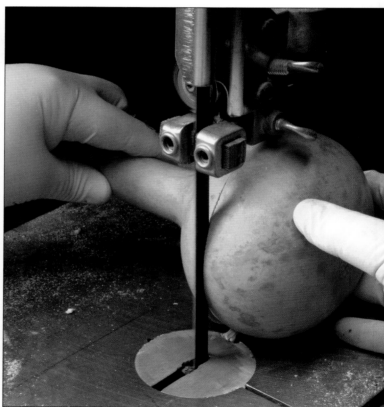

Pass the gourd through the blade in one swipe. Do not back up.

Turn on the bandsaw.

Once the gourd is through the blade, let the halves fall apart, allowing the interior loose stuff fall where it might.

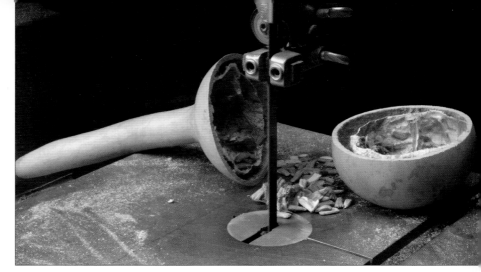

Turn off the bandsaw.

Once the bandsaw is completely at rest, reach for the gourd parts and seeds that fell out.

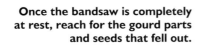

2121 Dakota Avenue
South Sioux City, NE 68776

Sanding Edges

Hand sanding will be the easiest way to touch up nicks and other odd or rough places when spot sanding a birdhouse hole or a small piece of gourd. I use Sandblaster sandpaper because it doesn't clog and comes in bright colors. It costs a little more than regular sandpaper, but it lasts longer and I can find it quickly among the piles of gourd colored scraps on my workbench.

Whole rims can be hand-sanded by stroking the edge with sandpaper, or by taping a full piece of sandpaper to a flat surface and rubbing the gourd's rim on it in a circular motion.

By far, the fastest way to finish several rims and get them level - whether they were cut with hand tools, a jigsaw, or a bandsaw - is with a belt sander. Belt sanders are fast, complete, and inexpensive as far as power tools go. Note: They will also produce such a mess of fine gourd dust you should consider only using this tool outside in a breeze.

Whatever methods you use for sanding the edges of your gourds, just make sure to wear a respirator and safety goggles. As stated earlier, gourd dust is toxic and a little will go a long way, whether you sand with a sandpaper or power tool.

Let's be safe!

Here we are sanding the curvy rim for the jar we cut earlier. Careful sanding, all along the rim or just in spots, allows for slow control of the amount of material being abraided away.

Jagged or rough edges of a gourd can be smoothed by rubbing the whole edge of an opened gourd on a piece of sandpaper taped to a flat surface; this will produce a flat rim.

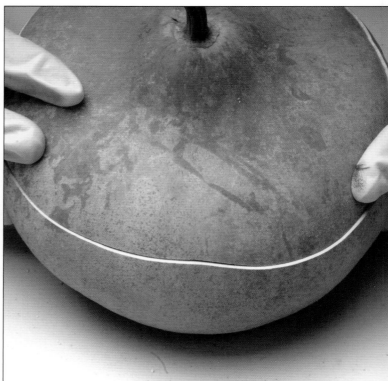

When making a gourd jar, sand only enough to get a smoother edge because overzealous sanding will take away too much of the line where the lid meets the bowl.

A nice fit.

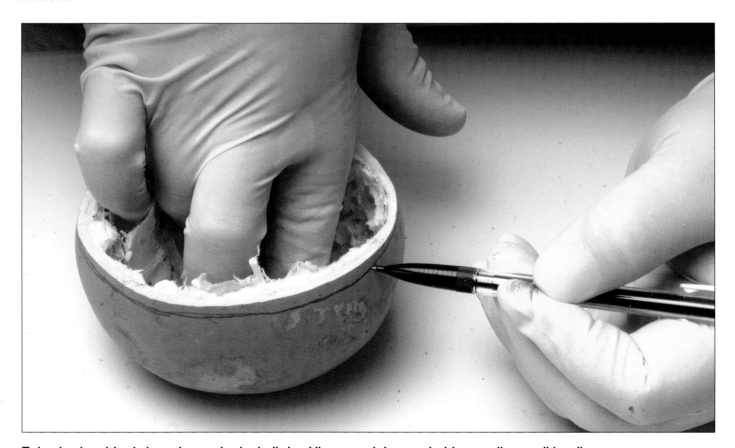

To level a rim with a belt sander, mark a basically level line around the gourd with a pencil as we did earlier to indicate a sanding boundary.

Turn the belt sander on and hold the gourd with two hands.

In small turning increments, move the gourd around and around with the rim against the belt.

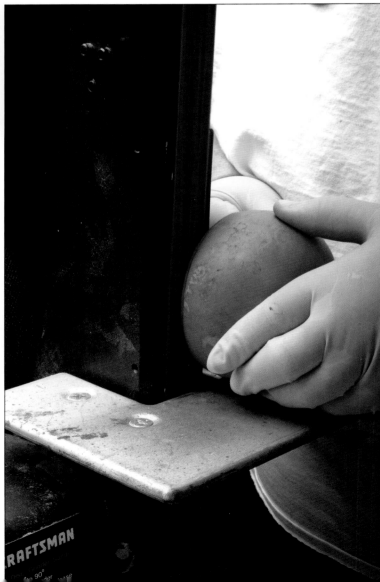

Turn off sander and set the bowl on a table. Critically check the rim for a level appearance.

Re-sand as needed, until level.

Part Four:

Gutting the Gourds

Rough Gutting

Some gourds will only need rough gutting before continuing with a project. Examples of this include bowls you intend to line with cloth and gourd birdhouses among other things. 'Rough gutting' is the scraping of seeds and connective tissue from the interior gourd wall, then shaking or vacuuming out any leftover bits. Seeds can be planted if they have not been frozen and are not molded or rotten.

They can also be used in decorative ways for gourd projects such as shingles on a gourd dollhouse or as beads in a gourd necklace.

Let's grab some big stuff out of a gourd!

Some interiors will have lovely seeds and white pith.

Some interiors will not be pretty at all!

Open a gourd and take off the top, exposing the interior.

Loosen the big debris and empty.

Using a grapefruit spoon or another scraping tool, remove the big pieces of pith and seeds.

Vacuum the minor dust thoroughly.

With birdhouses, only the birds will see the interior and they will appreciate a little leftover debris for their nests. The challenge will be to get the inside debris out without completely opening the gourd and then having to re-glue it together later. A bit of patience is all you need.

Generally, I take a one-size-fits-all approach to birdhouses and produce entry holes that are about 7/8" for all small birds in my area. Cutting the hole with a drill equipped with a peephole cutter is fast, but hand twisting a large drill bit for a starter hole and then enlarging it with sanding works too.

Drill the hole for the house entry.

Choose a clean bottleneck gourd and mark a spot on the lower belly that is vertical to the hanging gourd. If the hole is too high, the rain gets in; if it's too low, the nest inhabitants are in jeopardy of falling out.

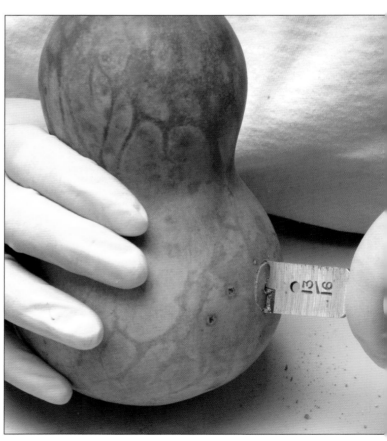

On the opposite side (for example purposes only), I am twisting a large drill bit to make the initial hole. If you use a drill, the spinning bit can be run in and out of the hole to enlarge it a little more.

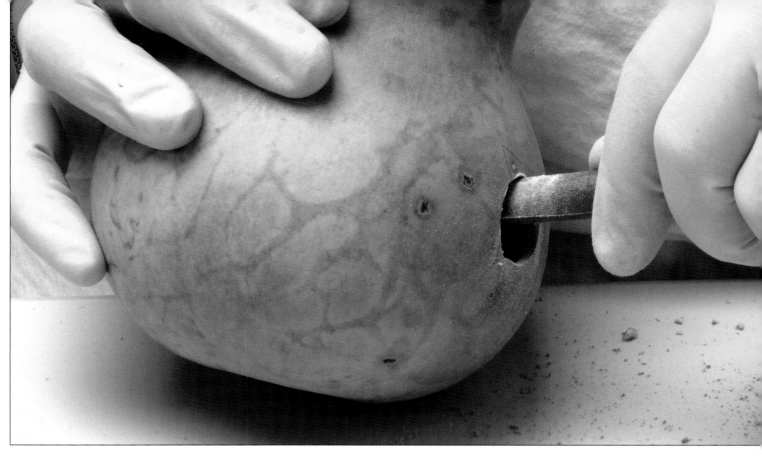

Wrapping a piece of sandpaper around a pencil and scraping around the hole will enlarge it.

Return to the original entry hole and shake out the loose interior debris of seeds and pith.

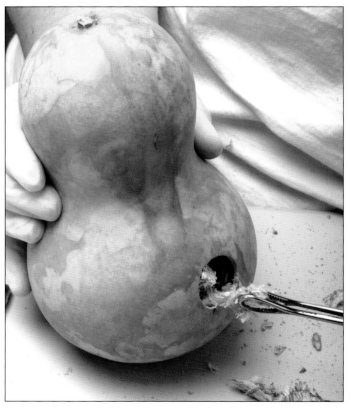

Using whatever grabbing tool you have, take out the bigger pieces of the interior.

Keep picking debris out of the gourd until nothing rattles and there seems to be an open area in the center for a nest.

Finish up by sanding the hole where it got knocked about during the debris-dragging stage.

Smooth Gutting

The mark of a lovely gourd project, in my opinion, is the care given to the inside of a piece of gourd art—the part not immediately seen. Like the stem, how the interior is finished indicates the creator's care and attention to detail.

A smooth interior, devoid of any leftover dehydrated debris, can be done by hand using simple household items to scrape pith from the interior wall of the gourd and then smoothing the surface with sandpaper.

Let's get smooth!

Begin with an opened and emptied gourd. Sometimes you get lucky and everything comes out in one lump.

Other times, a bit of work will be in order as you can see here—where the pith and some molded seeds are still connected to the wall.

Use a scraper (I have a grapefruit spoon) and remove as much debris as possible.

Empty the debris and use pliers to snap off the pointy, hard blossom end. It can be sanded away, but removing it is more efficient.

Scrape any odds and ends that remain.

Look... an empty gourd.

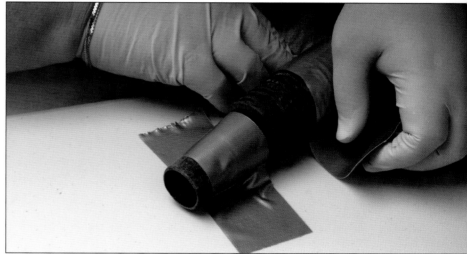

Set up a shop vacuum nearby so the nozzle is near the gourd to catch most of the dust as it becomes airborne. I have duct taped the nozzle onto the table where I am working.

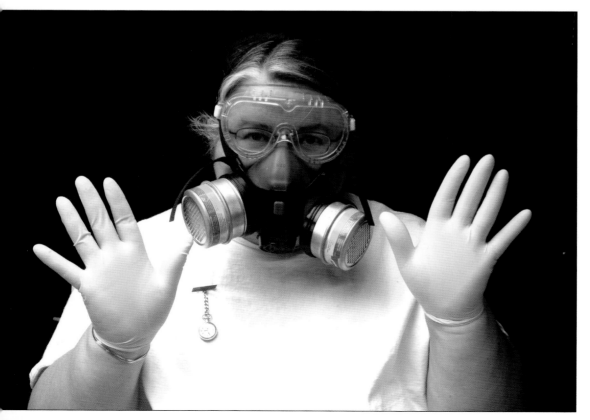

Don a respirator, safety goggles, and latex gloves because it is time to do some sanding to fine tune the gutting for a smooth finish.

After turning on the vacuum, start sanding the interior with long strokes from the center to the rim.

Continue all around the gourd until you attain the desired smoothness; empty the accumulated dust toward the shop vacuum nozzle.

Wiping around the rim with the sandpaper finishes the job nicely.

Brush and vacuum the interior to clear the last of the dust, then turn off the vacuum.

Viola!

Hand scraping and sanding works well for one or two gourds, but what if you need to crank out 20 or more gourds? Multiple projects needing smooth interiors would take quite a bit of time. When I get this busy, I roll out a drill press. There may be easier ways to gut dozens of gourds fast, but no one has told me of one yet. You will produce more dust than you can imagine with this technique, so arm yourself!

Let's power gut!

Gather the pile of opened gourds you want to gut.

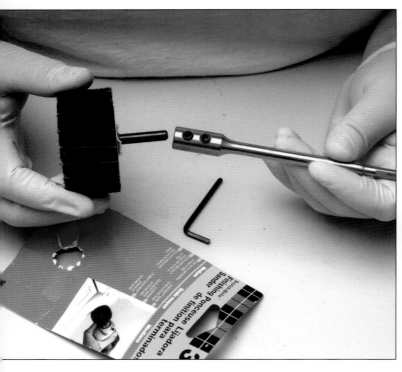

Attach a buffing sander (this is a **Scotch Brite** sanding bit) onto the end of a 6-inch extension arm.

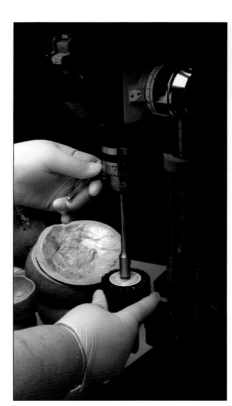

Insert the arm/ sander unit into the drill press. Note: The sanding attachment can be used on a regular hand drill, but you have to hold the drill with one hand as you hold the gourd with the other hand... challenging at best, and the source of hand cramps at worse.

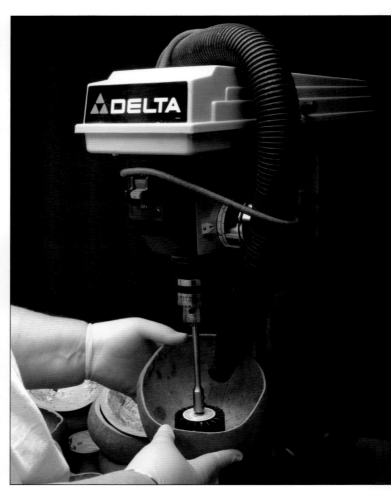

I usually arrange the shop vacuum near the drill press so the arm drapes over the top and lets the nozzle hang near the action to catch a lot of the dust as it appears. The amount of dust created with this technique can be overwhelming, especially when so many gourds are being done at once.

Don a respirator, safety goggles, and latex gloves. If you can take the drill press outside into a breeze, do so.

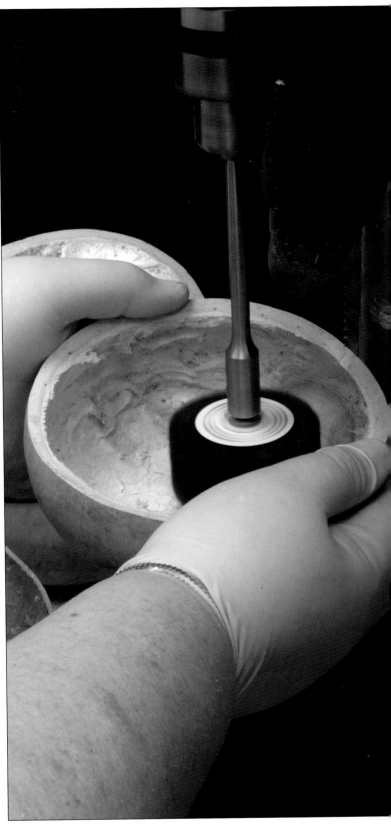

Turn on the drill press and position a gourd under the sanding bit.

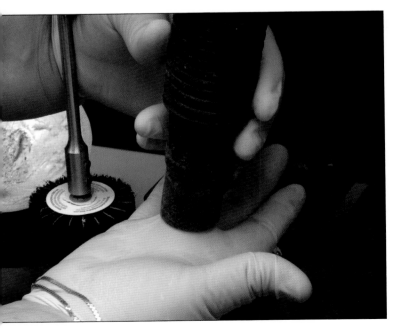

Turn on the vacuum.

With a slight pulling action, let the spinning sander run up the back of the gourd's interior.

Rotate the gourd a little and run the buffing sander up the back of the gourd's interior again.

Continue turning and gutting until the inside of the gourd is smooth.

Vacuum any dust residue out of the gourd.

SmoOOooooth!

Part Five:

Repairing the Accidents

Most gourd projects are durable for everyday use if treated like kitchen glassware...handled with some care, but still using it. Both unfinished and finished gourds with a waterproofing product can be rinsed and dried. Soaking would be a mistake for an unfinished gourd for obvious reasons, but soaking a waterproofed gourd should be discouraged also because a skipped spot in the seal will leave an area vulnerable to rot. Here at GourdGal manor, I use napkins or doilies to line plain, gutted and sanded gourds in the dining room for wrapped candies, bread, crackers, sugar packets, and fruit. Large gourds are used to store household things like seasonal linens, sewing projects, and studio tools. A quick wipe with a damp cloth cleans them nicely.

Cracks

Even though gourds are used as household and garden gadgets, they are not stainless steel and can crack if knocked against a hard surface with enough force. I have dropped gourd bowls on the garage floor and sometimes they have cracked, depending on how they landed. Gusts of wind have blown around gourds I was working on in the back yard and, though most survived, many cracked. These events are unfortunate, and elicit more than a few choice words, but cracks can usually be fixed.

Let's get crackin'!

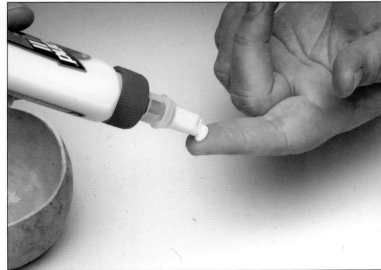

When a crack moves from the rim into the gourd...

...squeeze a drop of wood glue onto the tip of your finger...

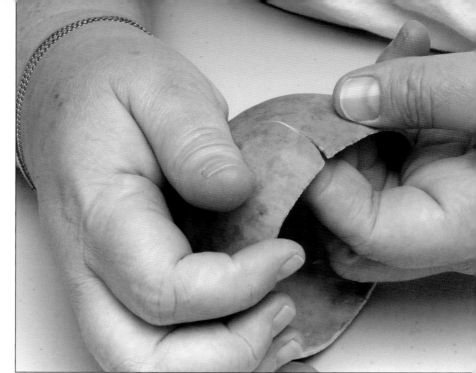

...and, spreading the crack slightly, press the glue into the crack from the interior.

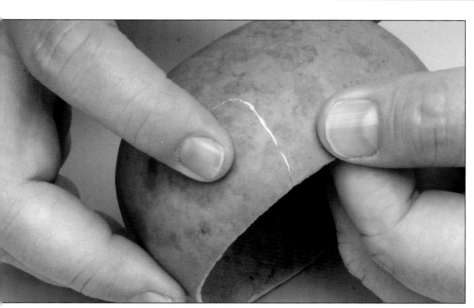

Allow the pressure of the gourd wall to pull the seam together.

If the sides of the seam do not align, clamp a clothespin at the rim to bring the two sides into position.

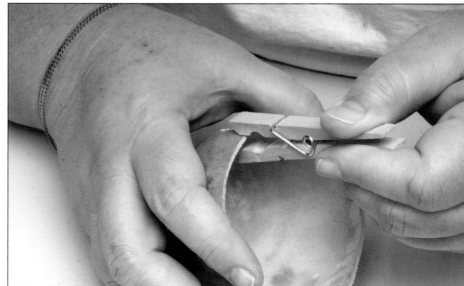

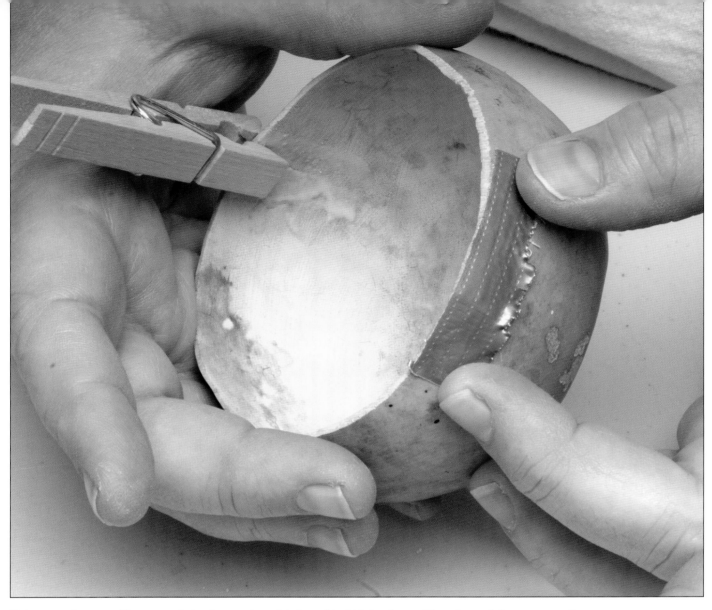

If the seam keeps pulling open, bring it together tightly and hold it in place with a piece of duct tape until the glue dries.

If glue oozes out of a seam being fixed, wipe with a damp cloth.

A more obvious, and sometimes decorative, crack mending technique is sewing the seam together with wire or leather. Start by drilling holes on either side of the crack.

Run a piece of wire through the holes as if lacing shoes. The crack still exists and can be seen, but depending on the wire you use, sewing can sometimes be the best part of the gourd!

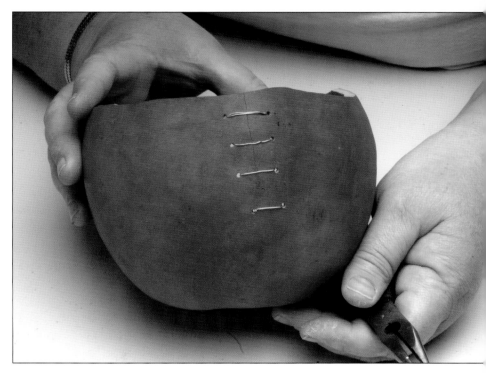

Leather looks good too and can be bought in many colors. Pictured, a repair sewn in leather.

Stems

Save all extra stems you come across whether you have an immediate use for them or not. Eventually, you will come across a gourd that is perfect in every way except it lacks a stem. Or, it has a stem but could use an unusual, curled, or twisted stem to bring out the best of its 'gourdiness'.

Let's attach a stem!

Start a repair to a detached stem, or to a stem you want to add to a stemless gourd, by boring a hole into the center of the stem with a darning needle, and another hole in the spot where the stem is to connect.

Squeeze a drop of wood glue into the stem hole and the gourd hole.

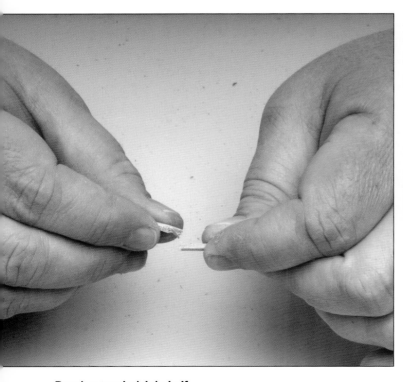

Break a toothpick in half.

46

Insert a piece of the toothpick into the holes, bringing the stem together with the gourd. Adjust the stem with a turn or jiggle to approximate an original position.

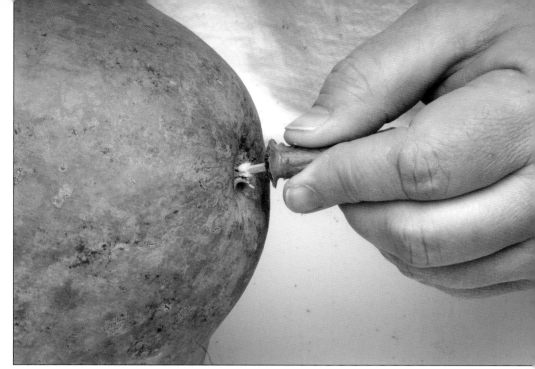

This process works well when turning a stem into a leg for a gourd that does not sit flat.

However, if the gourd wall is thin, the toothpick technique will not work. Instead, roughen the surface of the gourd with sandpaper.

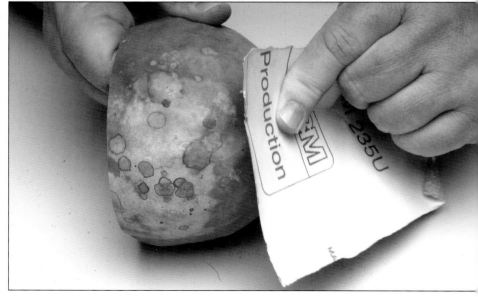

Sand and trim a stem to hug the gourd as if it actually grew out of the gourd wall.

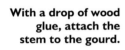

With a drop of wood glue, attach the stem to the gourd.

Use tape to hold the stem in place until the glue dries.

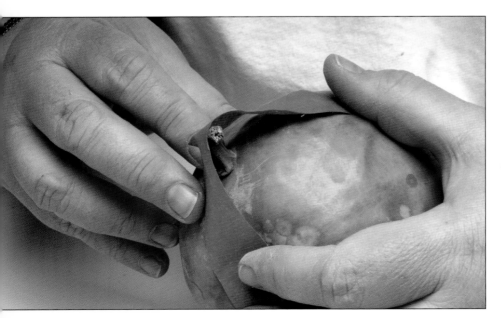

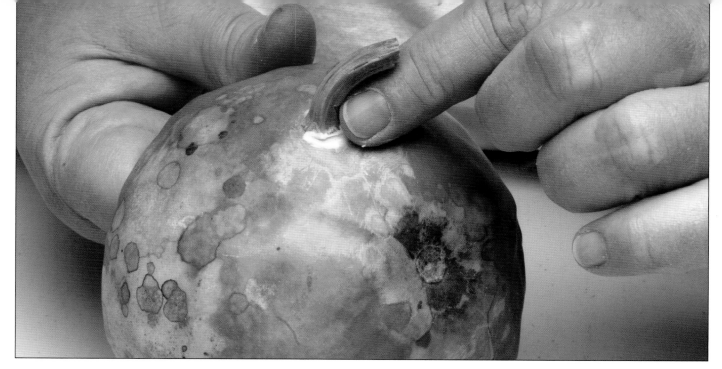

To reinforce, add a line of wood glue around the base of the leg where it connects to the gourd. Trim by running your fingertip along the line and let dry.

A broken stem can be fixed by squeezing glue into the crack and taping it in place until dry.

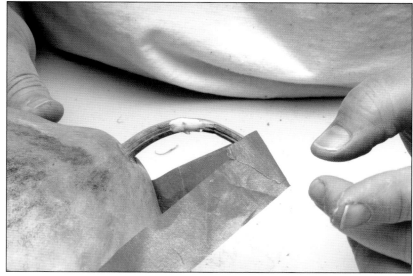

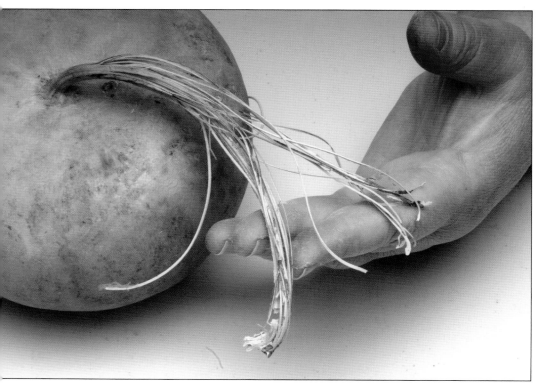

Repairing a shredded stem attached to its gourd can be a real test of will, but exciting! When doing this, I like to do more than one since a single effort will then pay off with multiple repairs.

Squeeze glue into the shredded pieces and bring them together until the original stem is duplicated.

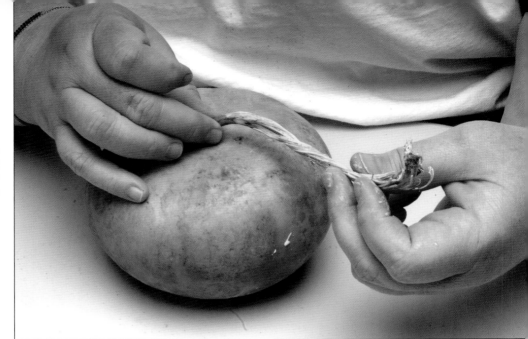

Wrap a piece of thin jewelry wire, fishing line, or tape around the stem in a candy-cane stripe fashion to hold the stem together while it dries.

Once dry, remove the retaining wire or string.

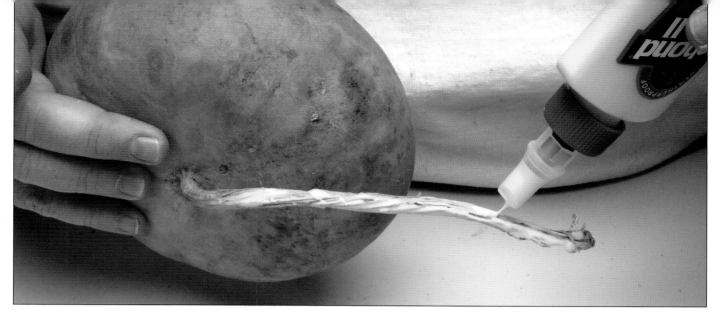

Dab glue into gaps that still exist. Let dry again.

Sand the rough spots left behind by the glue.

Eventually, you will have a reconstructed stem!

Walls

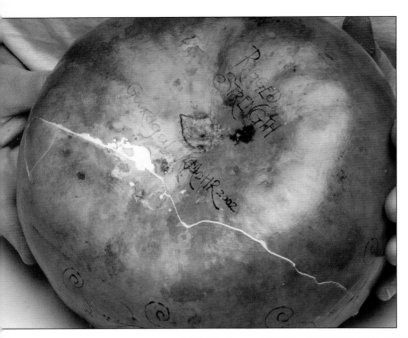

The large white area shows where the missing piece of wall was reconstructed.

On a similar note, a gourd that takes a hard hit and cracks, breaks, and loses pieces of its wall can be reconstructed also. Even a gourd that seemed promising at first, but when opened showed a thin spot or hole in the wall can be strengthened. The picture to the left is a gourd I accidentally ran over with my car. Luckily, it was not hit directly with the tires, but it did sustain cracks and lost some pieces of wall. A combination of wood glue and wood putty saved it, and I use it at the dinner table as a breadbasket.

Let's make a wall!

Here is a gourd needing repair: a crack with a hole...a crying shame.

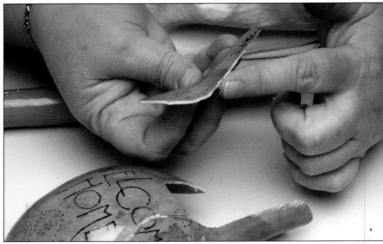

First, repair the crack with wood glue by pressing a dot of glue into the crack as described earlier.

Bring the cracked edges together and clamp with a clothespin and/or duct tape if necessary.

Continue building layers of putty until the hole is filled and is only slightly higher than the surrounding wall.

Once the glue has dried, spread a thin layer of wood putty across the hole and let dry. I use the pink putty that turns white as it dries because it is easy to know when I can layer more putty over the original layer or start sanding the area smooth, whichever is needed.

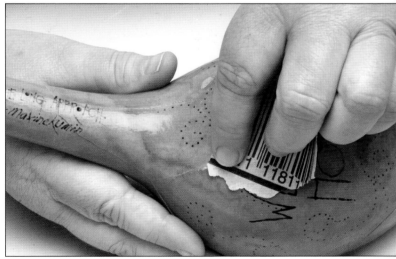

Sand the repair on both sides of the hole (interior and exterior gourd wall) until the putty is level with the surrounding wall, hopefully without sanding much of the gourd itself.

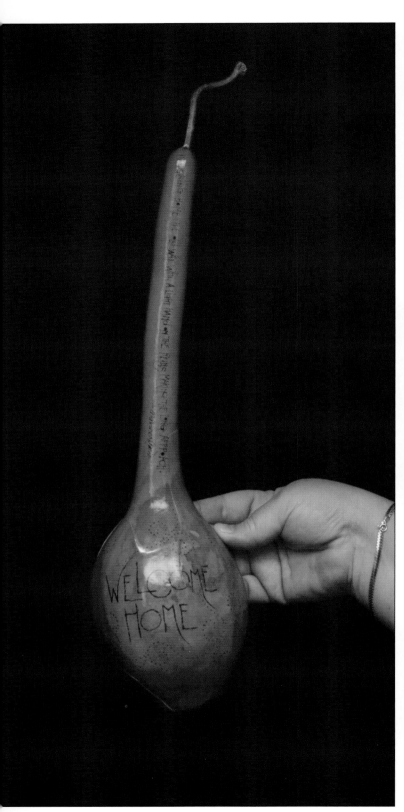

Now the gourd is ready to use again.

A thin spot in a gourd wall can be reinforced in similar fashion.

Spread a thin layer of wood putty across the thin spot.

Once dry, add another layer, making sure you feather the putty at the edges where the wall gets thicker. The goal is to add material to the thin spot, matching the thickness of the surrounding wall.

Eventually, the thin spot should be thick enough to match the surrounding wall.

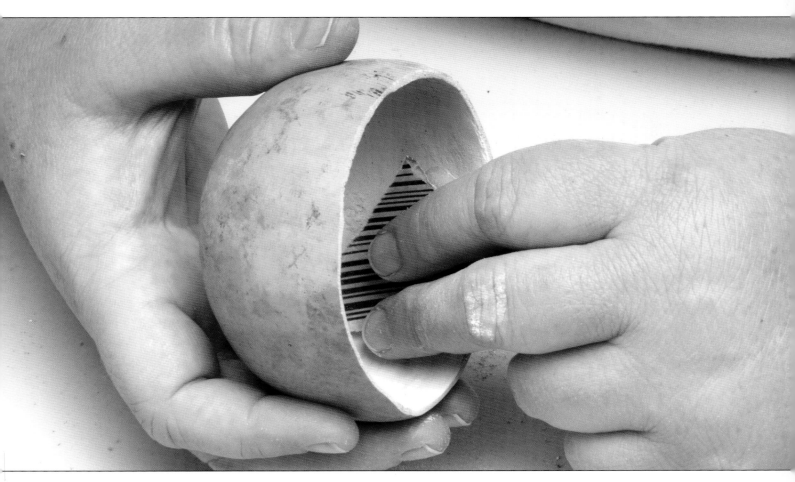

Sand the surface so the edges are indistinguishable from the surrounding wall. The color and texture differences will give the repair away, but they may not matter depending on how you finish the gourd.

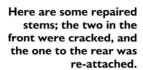

Here is a gourd with a crack that extended from the bottom to the rim of the bowl, shown here between index fingers.

Here are some repaired stems; the two in the front were cracked, and the one to the rear was re-attached.

Here is a gourd stem that was completely reconstructed.

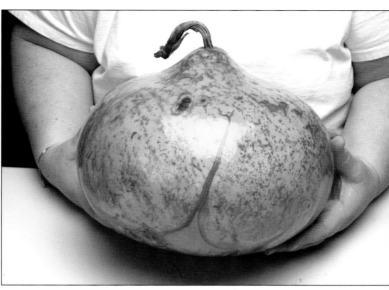

On this same gourd, the side had collapsed and was reconstructed with glue only.

Sometimes the mottled coloration on a gourd is so spectacular that it makes all repairs worthwhile.

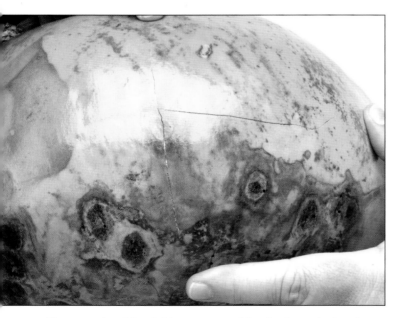

The opposite side of this same gourd has both vertical and horizontal cracks–also repaired with glue.

The crack on this previously-finished gourd was repaired and then colored with a permanent marker that had the same color as the gourd itself.

Conclusion

I am sure you have seen and learned something useful by now. I am equally sure I would see and learn something useful from you if I joined you in the garage next year at this time. That is the wonder and joy of "gourding" and, for gourd enthusiasts—the information builds and like-minded folk enjoy each other's company and knowledge. Investigate your local chapter of the American Gourd Society by going online to www.americangourdsociety.org and locate your state chapter. Many chapters can put you in touch with a nearby Gourd Patch, a subgroup of the state chapter arranged by county, town, or even neighborhoods depending on the numbers of gourders in the area.

Have a productive day and may the Good Gourd be yours!

Angela Mohr
GourdGal

Gallery

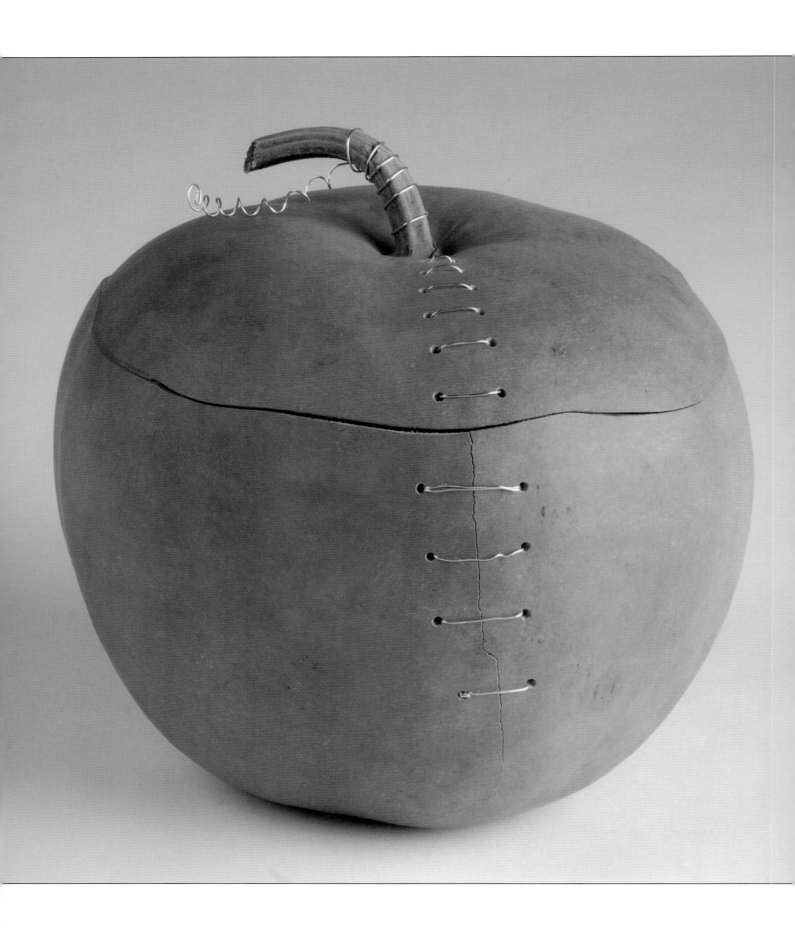

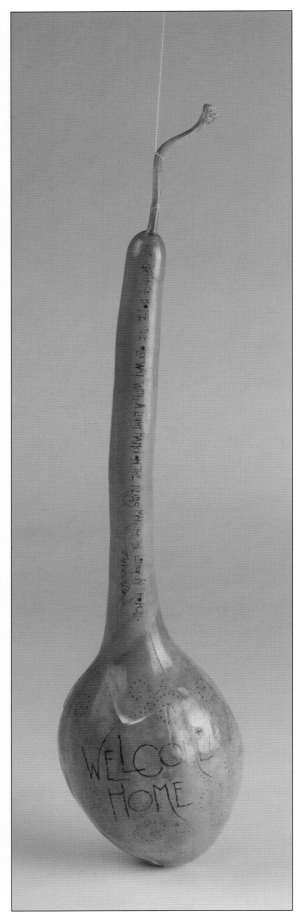

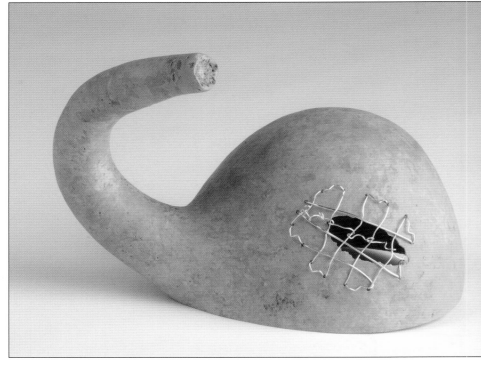